Under the Sea
Rays

by Jody Sullivan Rake

Consulting Editor: Gail Saunders-Smith, PhD

Consultant: Debbie Nuzzolo
Education Manager
SeaWorld, San Diego, California

Capstone
press

Mankato, Minnesota

Pebble Plus is published by Capstone Press,
151 Good Counsel Drive, P.O. Box 669, Mankato, Minnesota 56002.
www.capstonepress.com

1 2 3 4 5 6 11 10 09 08 07 06

Library of Congress Cataloging-in-Publication Data
Rake, Jody Sullivan.
 Rays / by Jody Sullivan Rake.
 p. cm.—(Pebble Plus. Under the sea)
 Summary: "Simple text and photographs present the lives of rays"—Provided by publisher.
 Includes bibliographical references and index.
 ISBN-13: 978-0-7368-6365-0 (hardcover)
 ISBN-10: 0-7368-6365-6 (hardcover)
 1. Rays (Fishes)—Juvenile literature. I. Title. II. Series: Under the sea (Mankato, Minn.)
 QL638.8.R35 2007
 597.3'5—dc22   2005035971

Editorial Credits
Mari Schuh, editor; Juliette Peters, set designer; Patrick D. Dentinger, book designer; Kelly Garvin,
 photo researcher

Photo Credits
Herb Segars, 17
Jeff Rotman, 5, 6–7, 13
Marty Snyderman, 14–15, 18–19
Nature Picture Library/Georgette Douwma, 20–21
PhotoDisc Inc., back cover
Seapics/Doug Perrine, 9, 10–11; Randy Morse, cover
Shutterstock/Brad Thompson, 1

Note to Parents and Teachers

The Under the Sea set supports national science standards related to the diversity and
unity of life. This book describes and illustrates rays. The images support early readers
in understanding the text. The repetition of words and phrases helps early readers learn
new words. This book also introduces early readers to subject-specific vocabulary words,
which are defined in the Glossary section. Early readers may need assistance to read
some words and to use the Table of Contents, Glossary, Read More, Internet Sites, and
Index sections of the book.

Table of Contents

What Are Rays?

Rays are fish
that are flat like pancakes.

Some rays are
as small as cookies.
Others are longer
than giraffes.

Body Parts

Rays have fins

that look like wings.

Rays move their fins to swim.

Rays have eyes

on top of their bodies.

A snout sticks out

in front of their eyes.

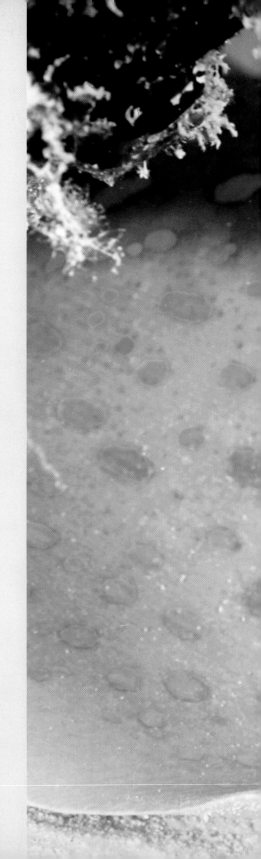

Rays have mouths

on the bottoms of their bodies.

Rows of hard teeth sit inside.

What Rays Do

Some rays eat squids, clams, and other shellfish. Rays crush their prey with their teeth.

Rays hide from predators
on the ocean floor.
They wiggle under the sand
with their fins.

Some rays sting predators
with the spines on their tails.

spine

Under the Sea

Rays glide

along the ocean floor.

Rays live under the sea.

Glossary

fin—a flat, flexible body part that helps ocean animals swim; rays have fins that look like wings.

glide—to move smoothly and easily

predator—an animal that hunts and eats other animals

prey—an animal that is eaten by another animal

shellfish—an ocean animal kept safe by a shell; clams, oysters, crabs, and snails are shellfish.

snout—the long front part of an animal's head

spine—a sharp, stiff, pointed part of a ray; rays sting predators with venom in their spine.

sting—to hurt with a venomous tip

Read More

Hirschmann, Kris. *Rays.* Creatures of the Sea. San Diego: Kidhaven Press, 2003.

Knox, Barbara. *ABC Under the Sea: An Ocean Life Alphabet Book.* Alphabet Books. Mankato, Minn.: A+ Books, 2003.

Walker, Sally M. *Rays.* Nature Watch. Minneapolis: Carolrhoda Books, 2003.

Internet Sites

FactHound offers a safe, fun way to find Internet sites related to this book. All of the sites on FactHound have been researched by our staff.

Here's how:

1. Visit *www.facthound.com*

2. Choose your grade level.

3. Type in this book ID **0736863656** for age-appropriate sites. You may also browse subjects by clicking on letters, or by clicking on pictures and words.

4. Click on the **Fetch It** button.

FactHound will fetch the best sites for you!

Index

Word Count: 117
Grade: 1
Early-Intervention Level: 12